ROXANA NASTASE

ENGLISH GRAMMAR
THE NOUN
EXPLANATIONS & EXERCISES
WITH ANSWERS

SCARLET LEAF

2017

*ENGLISH GRAMMAR PRACTICE – THE NOUN
EXPLANATIONS & EXERCISES WITH KEYS*

SCARLET LEAF PUBLISHING HOUSE

TORONTO

ONTARIO

CANADA

COPYRIGHT BY ROXANA NASTASE

ISBN: 978-1-988397-18-4

ENGLISH GRAMMAR PRACTICE – THE NOUN
EXPLANATIONS & EXERCISES WITH KEYS

All rights reserved. No part of this book can be used or reproduced in any manner whatsoever without written permission, except in the case of brief quotations embodied in critical articles and reviews.

For information address Scarlet Leaf Publishing House

Scarletleafpublishinghouse@gmail.com

Cover Design: Roxana Nastase

ENGLISH GRAMMAR PRACTICE – THE NOUN
EXPLANATIONS & EXERCISES WITH KEYS

UNIT 1: SINGULAR AND PLURAL OF THE NOUNS

RULES TO FORM THE PLURAL OF NOUNS

1. Most of the nouns add **–s** to singular to form the plural.

      Ex: chair → chair**s**

2. Nouns ending in **–ch, -sh, -s** or **–x** at singular, add **–es** for plural.

      Ex: watch → watch**es**

                 bush → bush**es**

                 kiss → kiss**es**

                 box → box**es**

*Note: the nouns POTATO and TOMATO add **-es** for plural:*

      potato → potato**es**

      tomato → tomato**es**

3. Nouns ending in a **consonant +-y** at singular turn **-y** into **-i** and add **-es** for plural.

      Ex: fly → fl**ies**

                try → tr**ies**

4. Nouns ending in **-f** or **-fe** at singular turn the respective termination into **-ves**.

      Ex: wolf → wol**ves**

                wife → wi**ves**

                leaf → leav**es**

                life → li**ves**

*Exception: **roof → roofs***

ENGLISH GRAMMAR PRACTICE – THE NOUN
EXPLANATIONS & EXERCISES WITH KEYS

5. Some nouns have irregular plural:

Ex:

man → men

child → children

woman → women

person → people

tooth → teeth

foot → feet

mouse → mice

sheep → sheep

fish → fish

ox → oxen

goose → geese

die → dice

NOTES:

1. Foreign nouns and abbreviations in –o add only –s at the form of the singular to form the plural.

Ex: photo → photos

piano → pianos

2. Names take –s for plural without modifications

Ex: Mary → Marys (The Marys of the world are too many to be counted)

3. Some nouns have the same form for the singular and the plural:

a) Some names of animals and fish

→ cod,   → plaice,

→ fish,   → trout,

→ mackerel,   → sheep,

→ salmon,   → deer,

→ pike,   → swine

b) Measurement units and numerals

→ Two hundred dollars

→ One dozen eggs - but two dozens eggs

c) *Nouns like: brace (= pair), yoke (= pair of oxen), stone (6.350 kg), couple, head, hundredweight (= 50 or 45 kg) are invariable after numerals and are always followed by **of***

Exceptions possible for:

pairs of; stone(s); hundredweight(s)

d) *The nouns: kind, sort, manner*

e) *Names of inhabitants of a country or towns that end in –e or –s:*

Ex: Chinese, Japanese, Portuguese, Viennese, Swiss

f) *The nouns:* **series** *and* **species**

4. We always use a verb in plural for:

a) *nouns like:*

cavalry	foot = infantry
gentry	craft = ships, boats
infantry	poultry
peasantry	clergy

nobility   horse = cavalry

laity   cattle

cannon

b) *adjectives and participle used as nouns like:*

the poor   the rich

the blind   the wounded

the accused   the deceased

5. *If we have an expression like:*

→ five pounds

→ ten liters

→ four miles

designating a quantity or a measurement unit, the verb will be used in singular.

Ex: Where's that two pounds I left on the table?

Ex: Four liters of milk is not enough.

6. The nouns people and police are always used with a verb in plural.

Ex: People are interesting.

Exception: when people represents a nation

Ex: The people of our country has made the choice.

Ex: The police are able to find the thief.

7. The following nouns are singular even though they end in -s:

Crossroads	Physics
News	Politics
Series	Economics
Means	Athletics
Mathematics	

Ex: Here's the news.

Ex: Physics is difficult.

UNIT 2: SINGULAR AND PLURAL OF THE NOUNS - PRACTICE

1. Rephrase the sentences using the nouns in plural instead of singular and make all necessary changes:

a) The table had only three legs.

_____

b) The boy played the piano in the sitting-room.

_____

c) The cat drank milk and washed itself afterwards.

_____

d) The chair was broken.

_____

e) He opened the window because it was too hot.

_____

f) The door was left open.

_____

g) The dog was barking while the chariot was passing by.

_____

h) The ashtray was full of ashes.

_____

i) The jar was in the pantry.

_____

j) The pen was lying on the floor.

_____

2. Fill in the blanks with one noun from the list; use the noun in singular or in plural, according to the meaning of the sentence:

bush, kiss, fly, potato, tooth, deer,

salmon, cavalry, news, Physics

a) She was listening to the _____ attentively and forgot everything about her _____ homework.

b) No one was touching the _____ on the table. They seemed weird and weren't appealing at all.

c) Their _____ were common knowledge. They could be seen kissing each other everywhere without concern about the people around.

d) The _____ attacked on the right flank and the horses came like a thunder from behind the _____.

e) He had to see the doctor. His _____ were painful and he couldn't chew anything at all.

f) The _____ were by the river drinking some water.

g) There were lots of _____ in the kitchen. Someone had forgotten to cover the jam jar.

h) I read that one can find _____ in these waters.

i) The _____ were hiding the house from the street.

j) She was choosing the _____. Most of them were too small and she was thinking with horror of peeling them.

3. Rephrase the following sentences putting the nouns in plural. Make all the necessary changes:

a) The watch was very expensive.

_____

b) The match was very exciting.

_____

c) The beach was full of shells.

_____

d) The sketch was very funny.

_____

e) The bitch barked at night and awaked everybody.

_____

f) The bush hid the view.

_____

g) The brush was green and silver.

_____

h) The dish was very tasty.

_____

i) They gave me a brush as a present.

_____

j) Joan left her watch on the night table.

_____

4. Rewrite the following sentences changing the singular of the nouns to plural and making all necessary changes to the sentences:

a) He read about an academy to see where he wanted to attend college.

_____

b) The dictionary was open on the desk where the girl left it before going out.

_____

c) Their activity was quite boring and the child couldn't understand how they could do it.

_____

d) That factory starts operation in June, they say.

_____

e) That family was quite wealthy.

_____

f) They revealed that conspiracy in due time.

_____

g) The lorry crashed into the walls of the building.

_____

h) The story captivated the child who was listening breathlessly.

_____

i) The county had a green field.

ENGLISH GRAMMAR PRACTICE – THE NOUN EXPLANATIONS & EXERCISES WITH KEYS

_____

j) The body lay on the kitchen floor when police came.

_____

5. Complete the following sentences using the words in brackets – use the noun in plural form and conjugate the verbs in the correct tense:

a) There _____ (be, **wife**) crying on the platform seeing off the soldiers.

b) The _____ (be, **knife**) silver and very sharp.

c) The _____ (run, **thief**) out of the shop after having been seen shoplifting.

d) The _____ (crash, **roof**) with noise.

e) The _____ (be, **calf**) delicate and funny.

f) The _____ (be, **scarf**) patterned and she liked them.

g) The _____`s (man, life)_____ (be) important to the general.

h) The _____ (be, leaf) rusty and yellow and autumn was in the air.

i) He heard _____ (wolf) in the forest near the village.

j) He took _____ (half) of the _____ (apple).

6. Rewrite the following sentences changing the singular form of the nouns to plural and making all necessary changes:

a) The box lay open near the wall.
_____

b) Fox is reddish and cunning.
_____

c) This tax is compulsory.
_____

d) The red dress is smart.
_____

e) The buss is full of people as you can see.
_____

f) He gave her a kiss and she blushed.
_____

g) The church was built in the 14th century.
_____

h) The couch is very comfortable.
_____

i) Gas is to be found everywhere in this area.
_____

j) The abyss is scary.

UNIT 3 – COMPOUND NOUNS

I. GENERAL NOTIONS

In English, we often put a noun before another one to form a compound noun. The first noun has almost the same function as an adjective (describes the second noun).

    Ex: a road map

             a business trip

Such nouns, that describe the noun following them, usually are at singular, even though the meaning is plural.

    Ex: a dog trainer

Some compound nouns are written with a dash in between, while others are written in one word. There is no general rule, so, the best way to find out how a compound noun is written is to use the dictionary.

II. PLURAL OF THE COMPOUND NOUNS

1) If both compounds of the compound noun are nouns, the prefix for plural is added to the second noun.

      Ex: bookcase → bookcases

             fellow-traveller → fellow-travellers

Exceptions:

a) If the first element of the compound noun is "man" or "woman" → both nouns will have a plural form

      Ex: man-servant → men-servants

b) When the first element is in genitive, we can put in plural only the possessor or both, depending on the meaning

      Ex: a man's house   → some men's houses

                              → some men's house

2) If the compound noun consists in a noun + prepositional phrase, then the noun is in plural

Ex: brother-in-law → brothers-in-law

3) When in the compound noun no one of the components is a noun, the last component will take the plural

Ex: grown-up → grown-ups

ENGLISH GRAMMAR PRACTICE – THE NOUN EXPLANATIONS & EXERCISES WITH KEYS

UNIT 4: SIMPLE NOUNS AND COMPOUND NOUNS PRACTICE

1. Rewrite the following sentences changing the singular of the nouns to plural. Don`t forget to make all the other necessary changes:

a) The child is in the house now so you shouldn`t worry anymore.

_____

b) I saw a pigeon on the gate when I came back home.

_____

c) He was looking at the passer-by when he saw the car.

_____

d) The woman bought a red hat and a coat.

_____

e) The goose was running around while the dog was barking.

_____

f) An ox was watching her across the field.

g) I get very well along with my sister-in-law.

_____

h) The box and the book were lying on the floor near the bed.

_____

i) I was watching a photo when he came.

_____

j) A man and a woman crossed the street when the policeman whistled.

_____

ENGLISH GRAMMAR PRACTICE – THE NOUN EXPLANATIONS & EXERCISES WITH KEYS

2. Rewrite the following sentences changing the nouns in plural to singular and make all necessary changes:

a) I watched the children playing in the garden all afternoon.

___

b) He entered the room and saw the women laughing.

___

c) There were some knives on the table.

___

d) His feet were hurt because he walked too much.

___

e) The cities came back to life again after the war.

___

f) There were some dry loaves of bread in the kitchen.

___

g) The shelves in the study were full of thick books.

___

h) No one saw those geese in their yard a few days ago.

___

i) Their brothers-in-law came to visit them.

___

j) The passers-by stopped when the cars started to move on.
_____

3. Fill in the blanks with the plural of the nouns given below:

brother-in-law; man; tomato; alley; woman; tooth; child; person; leaf; mouse; sheep

a) John told the _____ to behave.

b) Lucy and Ann saw the _____ along the road.

c) They decided to let their _____ to share their secret.

d) The _____ came out of his office shaking their hands.

e) The other day, we saw more _____ getting into that new bar.

f) You haven't chosen the good _____ for the salad.

g) The _____ have just fallen on the _____ of the park.

h) The _____ in the barn ate all the wheat.

i) I saw those _____ in that red car yesterday.

j) He took the brush from the shelf and brushed his _____.

4. Fill in the space with the following nouns in singular or plural, according to the meaning of the sentence:

appearance, grief, shoulder, woman, eye, mother, face, nightmare

a) She got up and she looked into the mirror. She realised at once that anybody could see the _____ on her _____.

b) No one could say that she wasn't a good _____. She looked after her children with a lot of patience and attention.

c) The _____ of the boy said one thing only: he had been in a fight.

d) Their _____ met and anybody could see their common interest.

e) It was a real _____. He couldn't have thought things could go so far.

f) The _____ looked at him and made a grimace. She didn't like his _____.

g) He had broad _____ and anyone was aware he was a strong man.

h) She was the only one who knew her _____. The others could only guess looking into her _____.

i) He could change his _____ at a whim. He liked keeping people on their toes.

j) The child had terrible _____ at night and his _____ didn't know what to do about.

5. Fill in the blanks using one noun from the list; use the noun either in singular or in plural, according to the meaning of the sentence:

hall, library, cat, boot, paper, smell, apartment, leather, tree, dressing-room

a) There were lots of _____ on the desk and he couldn't find the one he needed.

b) The _____ in the building were identical and if you had seen one, you'd have known how the others would look.

c) The _____ of the city offered several services especially for students.

d) He threw the _____ on the floor under the table. He was so tired after that long walk that he couldn't even look at them anymore.

e) There were lots of _____ in that house. It was the _____ of the dogs, mixing with the _____ of the _____ from the covers of the books in the _____ and the _____ of perfume from the _____.

f) The black _____ climbed the _____ in front of the bedroom window and the white _____ was lying in the sun on the verandah.

g) Her window was in the shadow of the _____ that were forming a small forest behind the house.

h) Dogs don't like _____ and that's almost an axiom. Our neighbour's dog chases our _____ all the time.

ENGLISH GRAMMAR PRACTICE – THE NOUN EXPLANATIONS & EXERCISES WITH KEYS

i) Mike's _____ were _____ _____ and their _____ was filling the small _____.

j) You should look through the _____ on the table in the _____. I think I saw it there.

UNIT 5: COUNTABLE AND UNCOUNTABLE NOUNS

1. Names of things, people, events etc. are countable nouns, because we can count them. → these nouns can have plural

Ex: a book → two books

*The indefinite article **a / an** can accompany such nouns when they have singular form.*

Note:

A - the word following the article starts with a consonant or a semi –vowel

    Ex: a horse

                a boy

                a red apple (*the adjective red is the word following the article, so the article will not be **an** for the apple*)

An - the word following the article starts with a vowel

Ex: an artist

an architect

Ex: an interesting car (*the adjective* interesting, *which starts with a vowel follows the article* → *the article is* **an**, *even though the noun starts with a consonant*)

2. Uncountable nouns designate nouns, concepts, etc., which cannot be divided in separate elements and therefore, cannot have plural.

Ex:

Music	Hair
Astonishment	Advice
Soap	News
Information	Knowledge
Milk	

Usually such nouns are often used with the article *some*:

Ex: some coffee

Uncountable nouns that should be known:

Air (the air we breathe)	Pepper
Sand	Butter
Advertising	Homework
News	Physics
Economics	Meat
Measles	Mathematics
Politics	Money
Soup	Soap
Spaghetti	Advice
Hair	Shampoo
Weather	Machinery
Travel (with the meaning of trip)	Knowledge
	Health
English	Furniture
French	Rice
Luggage	Rain
Oil	Salt
Petrol	Lemonade
Sugar	Curry
Juice	Marmalade

Note 1:

> advertising → uncountable noun
>
> advertisement → countable noun

> Ex: There are some interesting advertisements during this show.

Note 2: Some uncountable nouns can be used as countable nouns to indicate different types.

> Ex: food, meat, money, sand
>
> Ex 1: This is one of the foods I am not allowed to eat.

TIME → may be countable or uncountable, depending on the context:

1) If it refers to an occasion → countable noun

> Ex: He's visited us three times this month.

2) *If it refers to a number of hours, days, months, years etc.* → *an uncountable noun*

        Ex: You haven't spent too much time on your project.

Note 3:

*Nouns ending in **-ing** usually have a general meaning* → **uncountable**.

*However, they may have the meaning of a **countable** noun.*

        Ex: painting = art → **uncountable**

                painting – There are three paintings on the wall. → **countable**

UNIT 6: DETERMINANTS OF COUNTABLE AND UNCOUNTABLE NOUNS

1. A / An – indefinite article → used with nouns at singular

Ex: John has got a car.

   He's eating an apple.

2. Article Zero → used with countable and uncountable nouns

   Ex: John likes (_x_) cakes. (__x__) = *no article*

      cake – cakes → **countable noun**

   Ex: I prefer (__x__) honey. (__x__) = no article

      honey → **uncountable noun**

3. *Some* → used for countable and uncountable nouns when someone affirms something or requests or offers something

Any → used with both type of nouns when someone denies something and the verb is already in negative or when someone asks questions

Ex: I've got some juice but I haven't got any cakes.

You've got some glasses but have you got any cups?

Some is also used in questions when we ask something we already know about.

If the question begins with can/could then SOME is compulsory.

Ex 1: Have you got **some** news for me? (=actually, I think you might have)

Ex 2: Have you got **any** news for me? (= I'm asking but I don't know what answer you are going to give me)

Ex 3: Can / Could I have **some** more coffee, please?

Some uncountable nouns have a different meaning with a / an or some:

Ex: a coffee → a cup of coffee

some coffee → the material, the liquid with the name coffee

Ex: a fish → the fish as a being

some fish → a portion from some food

Ex: a glass → to drink from

some glass → glass as material; you can make a vase from it for instance

Ex: an iron → the one you use to iron clothes

some iron → the material from which you can make different tools for instance

Ex: a loaf (of bread) → that piece of bread, a baguette for instance, you buy from a store

some bread → material from which a loaf of bread is made

Ex: a paper → like a newspaper

some paper → material of which a piece of paper or a newspaper is made

Ex: a wood → like a small forest

some wood → the material, you can make a house of it for instance

→ a piece of wood

Some uncountable nouns used without article have a different meaning when they have *a / an* or *–s* for plural.

Ex: I can't stand noise. (*general*)

John has heard a strange noise. → *specific*

John keeps hearing noises. → *specific*

Some uncountable nouns can change their meaning when they are accompanied by a/an, however, they cannot have plural.

Ex: education → *in general*

a good education → *the period spent in school for instance*

4. Much / Many

MUCH is used for uncountable nouns.

MANY is used for countable nouns.

Both of them are used especially in questions and negative sentences → in affirmative, we prefer *a lot of / lots of* **instead of** *much / many.*

Ex:　　How much money have you got?

　　　　There isn't much good news today.

　　　　How many books are there?

　　　　There aren't many children in the classroom.

USE OF DETERMINANTS

With Countable Nouns (CN)	With Uncountable Nouns (UN)
a, the, some, any Ex: a book Ex: the book Ex: some books	**the, some, any** Ex: I drank the milk. *(there's none left)* Ex: I drank some milk. *(there's some milk left)* Ex: There isn't any sugar in this coffee.
this, that, these, those Ex: This book is good. (the book next to me or in my hand) Ex: That book is good. (the book is not near me) Ex: These books are good. (the books near me) Ex: Those books are good. (the books that are not near me)	**this, that → we use them when we understand the container, the cup etc.** Ex: This coffee is good. (the coffee in this cup, in other words) Ex: That milk is sour. (it is understood the milk in a cup or glass etc.)
none, one, two, three etc. Ex: None of the boys knows the answer. Ex: Four boys know the	**none** Ex: May I have a glass of milk, please? I have none.

answer.	
many → usually in negative and interrogative Ex: Are there many boys in here?	**much →** usually in negative and interrogative Ex: Is there much salt in the soup?
a lot of Ex: There are a lot of people in the house.	**a lot of** Ex: There is a lot of salt in the soup.
a large number of **a great number of** Ex: There are a large number of students in this hall. Ex: There are a great number of books.	**a large amount of** **a large quantity of** Ex: There's a large amount of coffee. Ex: There's a large quantity of coffee.
a few → approximation **few →** emphasis on the small number Ex: There are a few students in the room.	**a little →** approximation **little →** emphasis on the small quantity Ex: There's little sugar in this tea.
fewer ..... than Ex: There are fewer people in this shop than in the	**less .... than** Ex: There's less coffee in this cup than in the other one.

other one.	
more …… than	**more …… than**
Ex: There are more people in this room than in the next room.	Ex: There is more sugar in this bowl than in the other one.

UNIT 7: COUNTABLE AND UNCOUNTABLE NOUNS - PRACTICE

1. Which of the nouns below are countable and which are uncountable?

House _____

Water _____

Unhappiness _____

Cloud _____

Blood _____

Plastic _____

Car _____

Soap _____

Shoe _____

Battery _____

Cheese _____

Meat _____

Generosity _____

News _____
Pen _____
Shop _____
Window _____
Bread _____
Advice _____
Loaf _____

2. Choose the correct word underlined:

a) I've lost my luggage / luggages.

b) News is / are at eight o'clock.

c) Denise's hair / hairs is / are very long.

d) Could you help me with some advice / advices?

e) John and Ann will buy some new furniture / furnitures.

f) Alice needs some information / informations.

g) The / A milk is over.

h) The spaghetti is / are done.

i) I don't want to eat meat / meats at all.

j) I don't think that Alice's advice / advices is / are good.

3. Fill in the following sentences using one of the words from the list given (choose between their singular and plural form):

furniture, hair, news, information, advice, milk, Economy, juice, jam, spaghetti

a) I have bought some _____ and put it in my coffee.

b) There was _____ on the table besides butter and bread.

c) I cooked the _____ and then served dinner.

d) He was moving _____ around when Mary called on him.

e) I took the _____ he gave me and I succeeded.

f) They were looking for more _____ in that matter.

g) They studied _____ in faculty last year.

h) He broke the _____ to Ann last night.

i) He bought some _____ and left when we came in.

j) They went to have their _____ cut.

4. Choose the correct word or phrase underlined in each sentence:

a) How much / How many shoes have you got?

b) There are / There is some good news in the paper.

c) Spaghetti is / are good with tuna.

d) There is some / a glass on the table.

e) They gave her a / some good advice.

f) I have got some / any questions.

g) There isn't some / any milk in the fridge.

h) There was / were some information on the subject.

i) How much / How many money have you got on you?

j) Could I have some / any water, please?

5. Choose one word to fill in the blanks or leave the blank empty if the case is:

a) I need some pins. Have you got _____?

b) We need some bread. Could you go and buy _____ loaf?

c) Mary would like to get _____ news about that.

d) I haven't met him since _____ ages.

e) They don't have _____ good education.

f) I found _____ scissors under my table yesterday.

g) John didn't give me _____ good advice the other day.

h) My grandma has _____ very good health.

i) _____ knowledge of English is useful.

j) I bought _____ painting yesterday.

6. Complete the second sentence so that it has the same meaning as the first sentence and contains the word given:

a) Let me tell you what happened with them.

news

Let me _____

b) There isn't a lot of milk in the jug.

much

_____ milk in the jug.

c) I need some scissors here.

any

I haven't got _____.

d) John has to wash his clothes, I'm afraid.

washing

John's clothes _____.

e) We can't find our books.

where

_____ books?

f) The newspaper breaks no news on the subject.

in

The news _____.

g) What was the cost of your new car?

how

_____ your new car?

h) I must buy some bread for dinner.

any

_____ bread in my house.

i) Lucy has written me about her trip to Spain.

news

Lucy _____ about the trip in Spain.

j) Mary must go and cut her hair.

needs

_____ cutting.

7. Choose the correct variant:

a) She feels ill. She hasn't got _____.

1. a good health 2. good health

b) _____ money in my purse if you need some.

1. There is 2. There are

c) _____ students were there in the classroom?

1. How much 2. How many

d) I'd like _____ water.

1. a little 2. a few

e) Let John give you _____.

1. an advice 2. some advice

f) We've got _____ about the fire.

1. some news 2. a news

g) Taste the spaghetti! _____!

1. It's good 2. They're good

h) The neighbours have called the police and _____.

1. it's on its way 2. they're on their way

i) The room was full of _____.

1. a noise 2. noise

j) Juice? No, I haven't got _____.

1. any 2. some

8. Put one word in the blanks. If it is not possible to fill in the blank with a word leave it empty:

a) We'd like _____ coffee and _____ tea, please.

b) There is _____ coffee in the pot and _____ tea in _____ cups on the table.

c) He caught ____ big fish when he went fishing yesterday morning.

d) I'd like _____ fish and _____ boiled potatoes.

e) John broke _____ glass and _____ cups out of the four we had. Now we have only two cups.

f) We need _____ greenish glass for that vase.

g) Ask for _____ iron from Mrs. Smith so that I can iron your shirt.

h) This object is made of _____ iron.

i) This is _____ interesting paper and it presents _____ important news of the little town.

j) On the right side of the road, there was _____ small wood crossed by a stream.

9. **Fill in the blanks of the sentences below with one of the words or expressions from the following list:**

this, these, that, those, none, many, much, a lot of,

a few, a little

a) _____ coffee here is sweeter than _____ coffee there.

b) There were _____ people in the room, not many.

c) _____ of the boys had the book on the desk.

d) There was _____ salt in the soup, so I put some more.

e) _____ cups here are full but _____ cups there aren't.

f) Are there _____ boys in the room? No, there are only _____ boys.

g) There's _____ good food on the table.

h) There are _____ girls in the classroom but _____ boys.

i) There wasn't _____ news about the subject.

j) There isn't _____ tea left but there's _____ lemonade.

10. Fill in the blanks with one of the words or phrases in the list below; if no word or phrase is appropriate, leave the blank empty:

a large number of, more, many, few, any, a large amount of, much, the, no, some, fewer, less, some

a) There aren't _____ people in the show hall. There are _____ people. _____ people don't come to shows as they used to before.

b) There are _____ boys than girls in this room.

c) There's _____ furniture in this room than in the other one.

d) There's _____ rice on this plate than on that plate and I like _____ rice. _____ rice is very healthy.

e) There's _____ books to be read for this course.

f) They've brought _____ of soap in the harbour. I think we need _____ too.

g) There's not _____ useful information in this book.

h) He drank _____ coffee and there is _____ coffee left.

i) I don't have _____ book referring to this subject.

j) I ate _____ bread and butter. There is _____ _____ left on the table if you want.

UNIT 8: COLLECTIVE NOUNS

GENERAL NOTIONS

Many words indicating a number of people or animals are usually used at singular.

The following nouns are usually singular. We can consider them at plural, when we want to indicate that individual members act separately.

Ex:

Congress	jury
committee	organization
class	club
government	minority
army	team
majority*	crowd
family	public
group	

* **Majority** *can be singular or plural.*

If it is alone, then usually it followed by a verb in singular.

> Ex: The majority has voted the bill.

If it is followed by a noun in plural, then the verb will be in plural as well.

> Ex: The majority of the students have voted for John.

Note: *Some nouns expressing groups of people are used with the verb in plural even though they are singular.*

Ex: The government have decided

> → *however, it is possible to say also*: The government has decided

Ex: The police have come.

Ex: The team are confident.

The following expressions are used to express group of animals and therefore are considered singular:

        flock of birds   pack of wolves

        flock of sheep   school of fish

        herd of cattle   pride of lions

        pack of dogs

A NUMBER OF / THE NUMBER OF

A number of + noun in plural + verb plural

Ex: A number of students have come on time.

The number of students + noun in plural + verb singular

Ex: The number of students in this class has increased.

UNIT 9: COLLECTIVE NOUNS- PRACTICE

1. Fill in the blanks with one of the words in the list:

class, club, committee, crowd, group, jury, minority, majority, organization, team

a) The _____ declared that new rules would be adopted.

b) The _____ of the people in the room have approved the plan.

c) The _____ was pushing and yelling.

d) The _____ have reached a verdict.

e) The _____ took a trip to Niagara Falls last week.

f) The _____ has been defeated unfortunately.

g) Our _____ has had no chance to win.

h) Yesterday the _____ came up with the new rules.

i) The _____ fought bravely and won.

j) The chess _____ has organized a contest for next week.

2. Fill in the spaces with the words given:

flock, herd, pack, pride, school

a) The children were in the garden watching the _____ of birds in the sky.

b) The yacht-men saw a _____ of fish the other day.

c) The _____ of cattle passed across the village.

d) I saw a beautiful _____ of lions on TV yesterday.

e) The shepherd was young but he had his own _____ of sheep.

f) The child cried and said that a _____ of dogs chased it.

g) They knew that there was a _____ of wolves in the forest.

h) They showed a huge _____ of blue fish in that TV documentary.

i) The tourists admired the _____ of lions sleeping in the shadow.

j) The _____ of birds flew over the river.

3. Choose the correct word or phrase underlined in the following sentences:

a) A number of children has played / have played the ball.

b) The number of students is / are increasing nowadays.

c) The pack of wolves has attacked / have attacked the sheep.

d) The majority of the people has agreed / have agreed with the solution presented by John.

e) The public appreciates / appreciate such plays.

f) The school of small fish is / are chased by the big fish.

g) The number of problems has gathered / have gathered.

h) A herd of cattle was coming / were coming down the hill.

i) The majority of the women has / have black coats and hats.

j) The flock of sheep was eating / were eating grass while the shepherd was watching them.

4. Fill in the blanks with one of the words or phrases in the list below and put the verb in brackets at singular or plural, depending on the situation:

army, Congress, crowd, family, flock of birds, flock of sheep, pack of wolves, school of fish, a number of, the number of

a) The _____ (just, decide) to appoint a new candidate.

b) The _____ (just, gather) to discuss his problem.

c) The _____ (acclaim) while the star was passing through the people gathered to see him.

d) The _____ (just, decide) to change the uniforms.

e) The _____ (fly) south, while the little boy was watching the birds sadly. Summer had already passed.

f) The _____ (be) specific to the area.

g) The _____ (just, attack) the deer and put it down.

h) _____ of young people attending this specialization (decrease) lately.

i) _____ of books (recently, appear) on this subject.

j) The _____ (lie) in the shadow of the trees, while the shepherd was eating something nearby.

UNIT 10: NOUNS + PREPOSITIONS FOLLOWED BY GERUND

GENERAL NOTIONS

1. The following nouns + prepositions are always followed by gerund:

    choice of

    excuse for

    intention for

    method for/of

    possibility of

    reason for

    Ex: He had the choice of going there.

    Ex: We had the possibility of leaving earlier.

2. Other usual combinations noun + preposition:

equivalent of

example of

exception of

number of

quality of

pair of

sample of

3. The following nouns can be followed either by the preposition of or by the preposition for:

fear

hatred

means

method

need

Ex: The quality of this photo is not very different from that one. I saw a sample of his work and I was quite impressed.

UNIT 11: NOUNS + PREPOSITIONS FOLLOWED BY GERUND – PRACTICE

1. Fill in the blanks with the nouns + prepositions from the list and put the verbs in brackets to the correct form:

choice of, excuse for, intention of, method for/of, possibility of, reason for

a) George has no _____ (drop) out of school.

b) There is a _____ (acquire) this house at a good price.

c) There is no _____ (leave) this early.

d) They have developed a _____ (evaluate) the problem.

e) He has no _____ (go) there tonight.

f) We have no _____ (solve) the issue.

g) She has no _____ (turn) them down.

h) Sam has the _____ (leave) Sally for good.

i) We've got a strong _____ (make) this choice.

j) There's a _____ (find) the correct answer.

2. Rephrase the sentences using one of the phrases:

choice of, excuse for, intention of, method for, possibility of, reason for

a) He tried to find something to excuse himself because he failed in that matter.

_____

b) They looked for a way to get out of trouble.

_____

c) They shouldn't have left so early. They had no reason.

_____

d) She had to choose between the two places for spending the holiday.

_____

e) We had to find a way to solve the problem.

_____

f) He intended to go there.

_____

g) It was possible for them to take the exam.

_____

h) They had an explanation for what they had done.

_____

i) She wanted to move out of that house as soon as possible.

_____

j) They had their motives and therefore, they broke the deal.

_____

3. Rewrite the sentences using the word in brackets and keeping the meaning:

a) We shouldn't have done that. There was no reason, we know that. **(excuse)**

_____

b) They realised they couldn't get to a result with that man. **(possibility)**

_____

c) Alice was entitled to leave John. **(reasons)**

_____

d) I finally got to a way to apply my project. **(method)**

_____

e) They were determined to talk to him and solve that matter. **(intention)**

_____

f) Mary knew she could choose to come back any time. **(choice)**

_____

g) They found a better way to solve that situation. **(method)**

h) I don't think he could be excused for being there. **(excuse)**

i) I intend to write to him and ask him about everything. **(intention)**

j) The children could choose any of the main courses. **(possibility)**

UNIT 12: NOUNS FUNCTIONING AS ADJECTIVES

GENERAL NOTIONS

1. In English, many nouns may function as adjectives when they are used before other nouns. The first noun of the compound functions as an adjective and describes the second one, which functions as a noun.

2. The nouns functioning as adjectives are always in singular, even if they modify a noun in plural.

3. The combinations *numeral - noun* always are written with a dash in between.

Ex: We took a tour that lasted five weeks.

Ex: We took a five-week tour.

five-week → adjective   tour → noun

UNIT 13: NOUNS FUNCTIONING AS ADJECTIVES - PRACTICE

1. Fill in the second sentence so that it contains a noun from the first sentence but this time, the noun must function as an adjective. The meaning of the second sentence must be similar to the first one:

a) Mary's new flat is in a building, which has eight stories.

Mary's new flat is in _____ building.

b) They teach languages.

They are _____ teachers.

c) The girls saw a play in three acts last Sunday.

The girls saw a _____ play last Sunday.

d) The manager said that the sale would last for a week.

The manager said it would be _____ sale.

e) Delbert bought a kit containing twenty-eight pieces.

Delbert bought a _____ kit.

f) We have a bookcase with five shelves.

We have a _____ bookcase.

g) We need three cans of soup that weigh 250 grams each.

We need three _____ cans of soup.

h) They are experts in building houses made of bricks.

They are experts in building _____ houses.

i) Mr. Smith bought a bicycle with five speeds to his daughter yesterday.

Mr. Smith bought a _____ bicycle to his daughter yesterday.

j) The students wrote reports that were ten pages long.

The students wrote _____ reports.

2. Fill in the blanks with one of the words in the list below to obtain compound nouns:

ache, air, central, clip, glasses, lace, path, post, table, washing

a) He put the _____ cloth on the table.

b) The plane landed on the nearest _____ port due to damages.

c) He was wearing sun_____ because it was a very sunny and bright day.

d) She bought that neck_____ because it fitted her earrings.

e) He sent his letter by air _____.

f) He wrote everything down on the _____ board.

g) Both of them had horrible stomach - _____.

h) She put the clothes in the _____ - machine and turned it on.

i) It was too cold so they turned on the _____ heating.

j) That was the _____ way to Chatham.

3. Fill in the blanks with a word from the list to form compound nouns:

bathroom, bottle, central, door, dish, dryer, fiction, heating, hair, mirror, money, shed, science, screen, top, pocket, shop, television, washer, window

a) He never has enough _____ _____ to buy himself whatever he wants.

b) He unscrewed the _____ _____ and then drank directly from the bottle.

c) Jane took the _____ _____ to dry her hair.

d) They were watching the _____ _____ fascinated while people were passing by.

e) He was fond of _____ _____ and he read everything of this kind.

f) After finishing his job, he closed the _____ _____ behind.

g) The girl was watching herself in the _____ _____.

h) The house was warm and cozy due to the _____.

i) The _____ _____ was dusty and needed cleaning.

j) She put the dishes in the _____ and turned it on.

UNIT 14: SYNTHETIC GENITIVE (SAXON) AND ANALYTIC GENITIVE (LATIN)

SYNTHETIC GENITIVE (SAXON GENITIVE)

A. GENITIVE FOR SINGULAR

1. The genitive for singular is formed by adding 's after the possessor

Ex: The boy's car

   The boy's dog

   The boy's cars

   The boy's pens

   The boy's toys

2. The nouns ending in *-es [i:z]* at singular do not form synthetic genitive but only analytical genitive

   Ex: The part of Jeff Bridges

3. The name of classics and foreign names ending in *-s* add only the apostrophe:

    Ex: Dromichaetes' wars

             Socrates' works

4. The compound nouns or noun phrases are generally considered just one word:

    Ex: my father-in-law's job

             Stephen the Great's reign

             The man over there's wife

Note: If we want to show the different possessions of some people, we will use the apostrophe after each of them:

    Ex: Virginia Woolf's and Joyce's novels

Note the difference:

    Ex: Mr. and Mrs. Smith's son

5. For the compound nouns consisting in a ***noun + preposition***, we do not use genitive:

> Ex: looker-on

B. GENITIVE FOR PLURAL

1. To form the genitive for plural, we use only the apostrophe if the noun in plural ends in *-s*:

> Ex: the boys' car

2. If the noun in plural does not end in –s, then we use the apostrophe and *-s*:

> Ex: the men's car

3. The compound nouns that do not form the plural by adding –s at the last component of the compound, do not form synthetic genitive at plural:

> Ex: mothers-in-law

Special Situation

The apostrophe from genitive is often used to show that something is part of a certain thing:

    Ex: the book's cover

            the book's title

ANALYTIC GENITIVE (LATIN GENITIVE)

It is formed with the help of the preposition *of*, which is placed between the object someone possesses and the possessor:

    Ex: the leg of the table

Generally, we use it for objects and animals, as well as for the situations when we cannot use the synthetic genitive.

For people, we usually prefer the use of the synthetic genitive.

UNIT 15: SYNTHETIC AND ANALYTIC GENITIVE - PRACTICE

1. Put the apostrophe for the synthetic genitive where it is necessary:

a) The childrens ball is in the garden.

b) She took her mothers car and left.

c) We gave the girls books to their brothers.

d) The man over theres car is broken.

e) The boys cups are in the sink.

f) The womens houses are well cared of.

g) The birds feathers are red.

h) The girls dress is blue and white.

i) The teachers books are on his desk.

j) They took their friends notebooks to learn.

2. Fill in the second sentence so that it has the same meaning as the first sentence:

a) I tried to find the toys of the children.

_____ find the children _____.

b) The cars of the girls were in the parking lot.

The girls_____.

c) The ribbon of a girl was left in the dust of the road.

A girl_____.

d) The house of our cousin was quite roomy.

Our cousin_____.

e) The cover of the book was quite interesting.

The book_____.

f) The room of my brother is cozy and warm.

My _____.

g) The cup of my manager broke the other day.

My _____.

h) The bicycles of their sisters were in the garden.

Their _____.

i) She took the dress of her friend to go to a dance.

She took her _____.

j) I met the desk mate of my cousin yesterday.

I _____ desk mate yesterday.

ENGLISH GRAMMAR PRACTICE – THE NOUN EXPLANATIONS & EXERCISES WITH KEYS

3. Correct the mistakes in the following sentences:

a) The boys's car was broken on the side of the road when I passed by.

_____

b) They received their mother of letter yesterday morning.

_____.

c) She obliged their desk mates sister by doing that.

_____

d) We met our friend sister in the park the other day.

_____

e) Alice borrowed her brothers bike for a ride. She went to her friends house three blocks south.

_____

f) You took your sister cap by mistake, didn't you? It wasn't intentional.

_____

g) The two boys lived in their aunts house for two weeks because their parents were out of the country.

_____

h) I visited my grandparents farm last week and I had a lot of fun with our neighbours children.

_____

i) Mary understood her teachers explanation in class yesterday and therefore, she was able to help her friends sister.

_____

j) We gave them a lift in our father car last evening.

_____

4. Fill in the blanks using the words in brackets and the genitive:

a) The child was looking curiously at the _____ *(broken wing, bird)*.

b) The _____ was broken and we couldn't do anything. *(leg, table)*

c) The summer sun was shining brightly over the _____. *(fields, region)*

d) I saw _____ looking around with fear. *(eyes, deer)*

e) _____ was smart. *(dress, sister, your friend)*

f) _____ met the expectations. *(book, author)*

g) _____ was moving. *(solitude, young woman)*

h) _____ was open and we could look inside. *(door, room)*

i) _____ was strange and fascinating the same time. *(colour, shirt)*

j) _____ could be heard from the last floor. *(noise, street)*

5. Turn the analytic genitive into synthetic genitive where it is possible:

a) The book of the boy was lying on his desk during the class.

_____

b) They saw the new car of the young man in the street last night.

_____

c) The title of the book was exciting.

_____

d) The colour of the walls was white and blue.

_____

e) The wheel of the car came off.

_____

f) The sorrows of that man were beyond any imagination.

_____

g) He forgot the key of the door on his table at home.

_____

h) The name of the young actress was already famous.

_____

i) The desks of the classroom were new and clean.

_____

j) The situation of the trial wasn't settled up.

_____

UNIT 16: PROGRESSIVE TEST

1. Correct the mistakes in the following sentences:

a) The mans are in the sitting-room and they are talking to each other.

b) The shelfs are fool of jars of all sorts and all colours.

c) I got a lot of letter from my friends in the mountains during the last month.

d) Susan spoke to the childs and brought them sweets.

e) They brother-in-laws greeted the bride when she entered the hall.

f) The mouses ate the cheese in the pantry, I'm afraid.

g) He dropped the knifes while laying the table for the guests.

h) The boys offered some flower to their hostess.

i) The flys have come to the honey because they left the lid of the jar aside.

j) The gipsy settled their tents at the foot of the hill.

2. Fill in the blanks with the nouns in the brackets in plural form:

a) The _____ are playing in the park together with their _____. *(child, friend)*

b) When they left the _____, they left the _____ and _____ open. *(classroom, door, window)*

c) The ones that saw the _____ on the floor of the barn ran out screaming. *(mouse)*

d) The street was full of _____ and _____ having lively coloured _____ in their _____. *(man, woman, box, hand)*

e) The _____ with fine and golden sand were invaded by noisy _____. *(beach, person)*

f) From the top of the hill, you could see the _____ with red _____ and smoky _____. *(roof, tile, chimney)*

g) The _____ showed that they lost. *(die)*

h) Their yard was full of _____ and _____. *(goose, duck)*

i) The _____ were black and big. The _____ guarded them helped by three big _____. *(sheep, shepherd, dog)*

j) He was watching the _____ in the aquarium and enjoyed their _____ when three _____ came to him. *(fish, colour, man)*

3. Fill in the blanks with one word from the list below:

blue-jeans, children, government, Mathematics, matters, people, police, pounds, stories, team, teeth, trail, trousers

a) The _____ has decided to approve that move.

b) Do the three _____ belong to you?

c) My favourite subject is _____. Which is yours?

d) Where are my _____ _____?

e) _____ never understand such _____.

f) _____ abandoned that _____. They have new clues.

g) The _____ won the match on Saturday evening.

h) He never believed the _____ when he heard all those _____ they were saying.

i) They knew that they were in trouble when they saw _____ at their door.

j) He was a tall young man with big and white _____.

4. Choose the right answer to complete the conversation:

a) Have you got some water, please? I'm really thirsty.

1. No, I'm sorry, I have some.
2. No, I'm sorry, I don't have any.

b) Now, everything will turn back to order.

1. The police has come.
2. The police have come.

c) What do you think of the number of thefts in the area this year?

1. The number of thefts has increased.
2. The number of thefts have increased.

d) Who's that lady over there?

1. That one? She's George's aunt's daughter.
2. That one? She's the daughter of George's aunt.

e) How long did your trip take?

1. It's been a five-hours trip.
2. It's been a five-hour trip.

f) I've just seen Andrew. He seemed extremely upset.

1. Oh, don't you know? He's just lost his possibility to be elected president again.

2. Oh, don't you know? He's just lost his possibility of being elected president again.

g) I think we need more glasses for the reception, dear.

1. No, darling, we need less.

2. No, darling we need fewer.

h) Is there any sugar in this house?

1. No, I'm afraid there isn't any.

2. No, I'm afraid there isn't none.

i) Is there any coffee left after the meeting?

1. Oh, yes, there's a large amount of coffee, if you want some.

2. Oh, yes, there's a large number of coffee, if you want some.

j) What would you like to serve, sir?

1. I'd like a fish.

2. I'd like some fish.

5. Fill in the blanks with one of the words given in the list below:

any, none, few, fewer, less, little, more, some, the, that, this, those, two

a) _____ car here has a lower consumption than _____ car there.

b) _____ of the students knew the answer to the question and the teacher was very disappointed.

c) I have seen _____ people in the show-hall for this play than the other night.

d) I'd like _____ tea, if you don't mind. Not much, just a _____.

e) There's _____ understanding nowadays than it used to be before.

f) She ate _____ cake, I'm afraid. There's _____ left.

g) I need _____ pieces of meat not one, please.

h) There are _____ observations about that phenomenon, I'm afraid.

i) We need _____ information on the subject, to be sure.

j) They'd like _____ bread with their soup, auntie.

6. Fill in the blanks with one of the words or phrases given in the list below:

a coffee, a fish, a good education, a good health, a loaf, an iron, a noise, a wood, education, health, noise,

some bread, some coffee, some fish, some iron, wood

a) The people from table two would like _____.

b) _____ is important to make your way through life. However, to acquire _____ means a lot of work.

c) She is very sensitive. She can't stand _____.

d) She wished her aunt to enjoy _____. Her _____ wasn't what it used to be.

e) They woke up and listened attentively: _____ came from downstairs. One of them took a piece of _____ from the pile next to the fireplace.

f) She chose to eat _____ instead of soup.

g) Marian was sitting on the terrace with _____ in her hand and she was sipping the hot liquid now and then. She was watching _____ towers that could be seen in a distance.

h) They went shopping because they needed _____ to take care of their clothes. They also needed to buy _____.

i) It was just _____ but they managed to get lost.

j) He was watching _____ swimming towards the luxuriant vegetation on the bottom of the aquarium.

7. Fill in the blanks with one of the words or phrases given in the list below:

a glass, a loaf, a paper, food, foods, meat, meats, some bread, some glass, some paper

a) He went to buy _____ to replace the windows.

b) The _____ in this shop are always fresh. The butcher is a very attentive merchant.

c) She bought _____ and hurriedly opened it on page five to see the article about which everybody was talking.

d) _____ shouldn't be eaten so often, or at least that's what the people say.

e) There was a lot of _____ on the table and the four guests were wondering what was in their host's mind.

f) She needed _____ to print those invitations.

g) The child broke _____ while trying to pour some juice.

h) We need _____, I'm afraid, so Janice went out to buy _____. She must come back soon.

i) There are lots of _____ in this shop. You can choose one with _____, if you want.

j) I need _____ to write down a few facts.

KEY OF THE EXERCISES

UNIT 2: SINGULAR AND PLURAL OF THE NOUNS - PRACTICE

1. Rephrase the sentences using the nouns in plural instead of singular:

a) The tables had only three legs.

b) The boys played the pianos in the sitting-rooms.

c) The cats drank milk and washed themselves afterwards.

d) The chairs were broken.

e) He opened the windows because it was too hot.

f) The doors were left open.

g) The dogs were barking while the chariots were passing by.

h) The ashtrays were full of ashes.

i) The jars were in the pantries.

j) The pens were lying on the floor.

2. Fill in the blanks with one noun from the list; use the noun in singular or in plural, according to the meaning of the sentence:

bush, kiss, fly, potato, tooth, deer, salmon, cavalry, news, physics

a) She was listening to the news attentively and forgot everything about her Physics homework.

b) No one was touching the potatoes on the table. They seemed weird and weren't appealing at all.

c) Their kisses were common knowledge. They could be seen kissing each other everywhere without concern about the people around.

d) The cavalry attacked on the right flank and the horses came like a thunder from behind the bushes.

e) He had to see the doctor. His teeth were painful and he couldn't chew anything at all.

f) The deer were by the river drinking some water.

g) There were lots of flies in the kitchen. Someone had forgotten to cover the jam jar.

h) I read that one can find salmon in these waters.

i) The bushes were hiding the house from the street.

j) She was choosing the potatoes. Most of them were too small and she was thinking with horror of peeling them.

3. Rephrase the following sentences putting the nouns in plural. Do all the necessary changes:

a) The watches were very expensive.

b) The matches were very exciting.

c) The beaches were full of shells.

d) The sketches were very funny.

e) The bitches barked at night and awaked everybody.

f) The bushes hid the view.

g) The brushes were green and silver.

h) The dishes were very tasty.

i) They gave me some brushes as a present.

j) Joan left her watches on the night table.

4. Rewrite the following sentences changing the singular of the nouns to plural and making all necessary changes to the sentences:

a) He read about some academies to see where he wanted to attend college.

b) The dictionaries were open on the desk where the girl left them before going out.

c) Their activities were quite boring and the child couldn't understand how they could do it.

d) Those factories start operation in June, they say.

e) Those families were quite wealthy.

f) They revealed those conspiracies in due time.

g) The lorries crashed into the walls of the building.

h) The stories captivated the child who was listening breathlessly.

i) The counties had green fields.

j) The bodies lay on the kitchen floor when police came.

5. *Complete the following sentences using the words in brackets – use the noun in plural form and conjugate the verbs in the correct tense:*

a) There were wives crying on the platform seeing off the soldiers.

b) The knives were silver and very sharp.

c) The thieves ran out of the shop after having been seen shoplifting.

d) The roofs crashed with noise.

e) The calves were delicate and funny.

f) The scarves were patterned and she liked them.

g) The men`s lives were important to the general.

h) The leaves were rusty and yellow and autumn was in the air.

i) He heard wolves in the forest near the village.

j) He took half of the apples.

6. Rewrite the following sentences changing the singular form of the nouns to plural and making all necessary changes:

a) The boxes lay open near the wall.

b) Foxes are reddish and cunning.

c) These taxes are compulsory.

d) The red dresses are smart.

e) The busses are full of people as you can see.

f) He gave her some kisses and she blushed.

g) The churches were built in the 14th century.

h) The couches are very comfortable.

i) Gases are to be found everywhere in this area.

j) The abysses are scary.

UNIT 4: SIMPLE NOUNS AND COMPOUND NOUNS - PRACTICE

1. Rewrite the following sentences changing the singular of the nouns to plural. Don`t forget to make all the other necessary changes:

a) The children are in the house now so you shouldn`t worry anymore.

b) I saw some pigeons on the gates when I came back home.

c) He was looking at the passers-by when he saw the cars.

d) The women bought red hats and coats.

e) The geese were running around while the dogs were barking.

f) Some oxen were watching her across the fields.

g) I get very well along with my sisters-in-law.

h) The boxes and the books were lying on the floor near the bed.

i) I was watching some photos when he came.

j) Some men and women crossed the street when the policeman whistled.

2. Rewrite the following sentences changing the nouns in plural to singular and make all necessary changes:

a) I watched the child playing in the garden all afternoon.

b) He entered the room and saw the woman laughing.

c) There was a knife on the table.

d) His foot was hurt because he walked too much.

e) The city came back to life again after the war.

f) There was a dry loaf of bread in the kitchen.

g) The shelf in the study was full of thick books.

h) No one saw that goose in their yard a few days ago.

i) Their brother-in-law came to visit them.

j) The passer-by stopped when the car started to move on.

3. Fill in the blanks with the plural of the nouns given below:

brother-in-law; man; tomato; alley; woman; tooth; child; person; leaf; mouse; sheep

a) John told the children to behave.

b) Lucy and Ann saw the sheep along the road.

c) They decided to let their brothers-in-law to share their secret.

d) The men came out of his office shaking their hands.

e) The other day, we saw more people getting into that new bar.

f) You haven't chosen the good tomatoes for the salad.

g) The leaves have just fallen on the alleys of the park.

h) The mice in the barn ate all the wheat.

i) I saw those women in that red car yesterday.

j) He took the brush from the shelf and brushed his teeth.

4. Fill in the space with the following nouns in singular or plural, according to the meaning of the sentence:

appearance, grief, shoulder, woman, eye, mother, face, nightmare

a) She got up and she looked into the mirror. She realised at once that anybody could see the grief on her eyes.

b) No one could say that she wasn't a good mother. She looked after her children with a lot of patience and attention.

c) The appearance of the boy said one thing only: he had been in a fight.

d) Their eyes met and anybody could see their common interest.

e) It was a real nightmare. He couldn't have thought things could go so far.

f) The woman looked at him and made a grimace. She didn't like his appearance.

g) He had broad shoulders and anyone was aware he was a strong man.

h) She was the only one who knew her gried. The others could only guess looking into her eyes.

i) He could change his appearance at a whim. He liked keeping people on their toes.

j) The child had terrible nightmares at night and his mother didn't know what to do about.

5. Fill in the blanks using one noun from the list; use the noun either in singular or in plural, according to the meaning of the sentence:

hall, library, cat, boot, paper, smell, apartment, leather, tree, dressing-room

a) There were lots of papers on the desk and he couldn't find the one he needed.

b) The apartments in the building were identical and if you had seen one, you'd have known how the others would look.

c) The libraries of the city offered several services especially for students.

d) He threw the boots on the floor under the table. He was so tired after that long walk that he couldn't even look at them anymore.

e) There were lots of smells in that house. It was the smell of the dogs, mixing with the smell of the leather from the covers of the books in the library and the smell of perfume from the dressing-room.

f) The black cat climbed the tree in front of the bedroom window and the white cat was lying in the sun on the verandah.

g) Her window was in the shadow of the trees that were forming a small forest behind the house.

h) Dogs don't like cats and that's almost an axiom. Our neighbour's dog chases our cats all the time.

i) Mike's boots were leather boots and their smell was filling the small hall.

j) You should look through the papers on the table in the library. I think I saw it there.

UNIT 7: COUNTABLE AND UNCOUNTABLE NOUNS - PRACTICE

1. Which of the nouns below are countable and which are uncountable?

House → countable

Water → uncountable (with one exception ☐ ex: territorial waters)

Unhappiness → uncountable

Cloud → countable

Blood → uncountable

Plastic → uncountable

Car → countable

Soap → uncountable

Shoe → countable

Battery → countable

Cheese → uncountable

Meat → uncountable (with one exception → types of meat)

Generosity → uncountable

News → uncountable

Pen → countable

Shop → countable

Window → countable

Bread → uncountable

Advice → uncountable

Loaf → countable

2. Choose the correct word underlined:

a) I've lost my luggage.

b) News is at eight o'clock.

c) Denise's hair is very long.

d) Could you help me with some advice?

e) John and Ann will buy some new furniture.

f) Alice needs some information.

g) The milk is over.

h) The spaghetti is done.

i) I don't want to eat meat at all.

j) I don't think that Alice's advice is good.

3. Fill in the following sentences using one of the words from the list given (choose between their singular and plural form):

furniture, hair, news, information, advice, milk, Economy, juice, jam, spaghetti

a) I have bought some milk and put it in my coffee.

b) There was jam on the table besides butter and bread.

c) I cooked the spaghetti and then served dinner.

d) He was moving furniture around when Mary called on him.

e) I took the advice he gave me and I succeeded.

f) They were looking for more information in that matter.

g) They studied Economy in faculty last year.

h) He broke the news to Ann last night.

i) He bought some juice and left when we came in.

j) They went to have their hair cut.

4. Choose the correct word or phrase underlined in each sentence:

a) How many shoes have you got?

b) There is some good news in the paper.

c) Spaghetti is good with tuna.

d) There is a glass on the table.

e) They gave her some good advice.

f) I have got some questions.

g) There isn't any milk in the fridge.

h) There was some information on the subject.

i) How much money have you got on you?

j) Could I have some water, please?

5. Choose one word to fill in the blanks or leave the blank empty if the case is:

a) I need some pins. Have you got any?

b) We need some bread. Could you go and buy a loaf?

c) Mary would like to get some news about that.

d) I haven't met him since ages.

e) They don't have a good education.

f) I found some scissors under my table yesterday.

g) John didn't give me good advice the other day.

h) My grandma has a very good health.

i) Knowledge of English is useful.

j) I bought a painting yesterday.

6. Complete the second sentence so that it has the same meaning as the first sentence and contains the word given:

a) Let me tell you the news about them.

b) There isn't much milk in the jug.

c) I haven't got any scissors and I need some.

d) John's clothes need washing, I'm afraid.

e) Where are our books?

f) The news about the subject is not in the newspaper.

g) How much was your new car?

h) I haven't got any bread in my house.

i) Lucy has sent me news about the trip in Spain.

j) Mary's hair needs cutting.

7. Choose the correct variant:

a) She feels ill. She hasn't got good health.

b) There is money in my purse if you need some.

c) How many students were there in the classroom?

d) I'd like a little water.

e) Let John give you some advice.

f) We've got some news about the fire.

g) Taste the spaghetti! It's good!

h) The neighbours have called the police and they're on their way.

i) The room was full of noise.

j) Juice? No, I haven't got any.

8. Put one word in the blanks. If it is not possible to fill in the blank with a word leave it empty:

a) We'd like a coffee and a tea, please.

b) There is some coffee in the pot and some tea in the cups on the table.

c) He caught a big fish when he went fishing yesterday morning.

d) I'd like some fish and some boiled potatoes.

e) John broke a glass and two cups out of the four we had. Now we have only two cups.

f) We need some greenish glass for that vase.

g) Ask for an iron from Mrs. Smith so that I can iron your shirt.

h) This object is made of iron.

i) This is an interesting paper and it presents the important news of the little town.

j) On the right side of the road, there was a small wood crossed by a stream.

9. *Fill in the blanks of the sentences below with one of the words or expressions from the following list:*

this, these, that, those, none, many, much, a lot of, a few, a little

a) This coffee here is sweeter than that coffee there.

b) There were a few people in the room, not many.

c) None of the boys had the book on the desk.

d) There was a little salt in the soup, so I put some more.

e) These cups here are full but those cups there aren't.

f) Are there many boys in the room? No, there are only a few boys.

g) There's a lot of good food on the table.

h) There are a lot of girls in the classroom but a few boys.

i) There wasn't much news about the subject.

j) There isn't much tea left but there's a lot of lemonade.

10. Fill in the blanks with one of the words or phrases in the list below; if no word or phrase is appropriate, leave the blank empty:

a large number of, more, many, few, any,

a large amount of, much, the, no, some, fewer, less, some

a) There aren't many people in the show hall. There are few people. People don't come to shows as they used to before.

b) There are fewer boys than girls in this room.

c) There's more furniture in this room than in the other one.

d) There's less rice on this plate than on that plate and I like more rice. Rice is very healthy.

e) There's a large number of books to be read for this course.

f) They've brought a large amount of soap in the harbour. I think we need some too.

g) There's not much useful information in this book.

h) He drank the coffee and there is no coffee left.

i) I don't have any book referring to this subject.

j) I ate some bread and butter. There is some more left on the table if you want.

UNIT 9: COLLECTIVE NOUNS - PRACTICE

1. Fill in the blanks with one of the words in the list:

class, club, committee, crowd, group, jury, minority, majority, organization, team

a) The committee declared that new rules would be adopted.

b) The majority of the people in the room have approved the plan.

c) The crowd was pushing and yelling.

d) The jury have reached a verdict.

e) The class took a trip to Niagara Falls last week.

f) The minority has been defeated unfortunately.

g) Our team has had no chance to win.

h) Yesterday the organization came up with the new rules.

i) The team fought bravely and won.

j) The chess club has organized a contest for next week.

2. Fill in the spaces with the words given:

flock, herd, pack, pride, school

a) The children were in the garden watching the flock of birds in the sky.

b) The yacht-men saw a school of fish the other day.

c) The herd of cattle passed across the village.

d) I saw a beautiful pride of lions on TV yesterday.

e) The shepherd was young but he had his own flock of sheep.

f) The child cried and said that a pack of dogs chased it.

g) They knew that there was a pack of wolves in the forest.

h) They showed a huge school of blue fish in that TV documentary.

i) The tourists admired the pride of lions sleeping in the shadow.

j) The flock of birds flew over the river.

3. Choose the correct word or phrase underlined in the following sentences:

a) A number of children have played the ball.

b) The number of students is increasing nowadays.

c) The pack of wolves has attacked the sheep.

d) The majority of the people have agreed with the solution presented by John.

e) The public appreciates such plays.

f) The school of small fish is by the big fish.

g) The number of problems has gathered.

h) A herd of cattle was coming down the hill.

i) The majority of the women have black coats and hats.

j) The flock of sheep was eating grass while the shepherd was watching them.

4. Fill in the blanks with one of the words or phrases in the list below and put the verb in brackets at singular or plural, depending on the situation:

army, Congress, crowd, family, flock of birds, flock of sheep, pack of wolves, school of fish, a number of, the number of

a) The Congress has just decided to appoint a new candidate.

b) The family has just gathered to discuss his problem.

c) The crows was acclaiming while the star was passing through the people gathered to see him.

d) The army has just decided to change the uniforms.

e) The flock of birds was flying south, while the little boy was watching the birds sadly. Summer had already passed.

f) The school of fish was specific to the area.

g) The pack of wolves has just attacked the deer and put it down.

h) The number of young people attending this specialization has decreased lately.

i) A number of books have recently appeared on this subject.

j) The flock of sheep was lying in the shadow of the trees, while the shepherd was eating something nearby.

UNIT 11: NOUNS + PREPOSITIONS FOLLOWED BY GERUND – PRACTICE

1. Fill in the blanks with the nouns + prepositions from the list and put the verbs in brackets to the correct form:

choice of, excuse for, intention of, method for/of, possibility of, reason for

a) George has no excuse for dropping out of school.

b) There is a possibility of acquiring this house at a good price.

c) There is no reason for leaving this early.

d) They have developed a method for evaluating the problem.

e) He has no intention of going there tonight.

f) We have no possibility of solving the issue.

g) She has no choice of turning them down.

h) Sam has the intention of leaving Sally for good.

i) We've got a strong reason for making this choice.

j) There's a method for finding the correct answer.

2. Rephrase the sentences using one of the phrases:

choice of, excuse for, intention of, method for, possibility of, reason for

a) He tried to find an excuse for failing that matter.

b) They looked for a possibility of getting out of trouble.

c) They had no reason for leaving so early.

d) She had a choice of spending her holiday in one of the two places.

e) We had to find a method for solving the problem.

f) He had the intention of going there.

g) They had the possibility of taking the exam.

h) They had an excuse for having done that.

i) She had the intention of moving out of that house as soon as possible.

j) They had the reasons for breaking the deal and they did it.

3. Rewrite the sentences using the word in brackets and keeping the meaning:

a) We had no excuse for having done that.

b) They didn't have the possibility of solving anything with that man. They were aware of that.

c) Alice had reasons for leaving John.

d) I finally found the method for applying my project.

e) They had the intention of talking to him and solving the problem.

f) Mary could have a choice of coming back any time.

g) They found a better method of solving that situation.

h) I don't think he has an excuse for having been there.

i) I have the intention of writing to him and asking him about everything.

j) The children had the possibility of choosing one of the main courses.

UNIT 13: NOUNS FUNCTIONING AS ADJECTIVES - PRACTICE

1. Fill in the second sentence so that it contains a noun from the first sentence but this time, the noun must function as an adjective. The meaning of the second sentence must be similar to the first one:

a) Mary's new flat is in an eight-storey building.

b) They are language teachers.

c) The girls saw a three-act play last Sunday.

d) The manager said it would be one-week sale.

e) Delbert bought a twenty-eight-piece kit.

f) We have a five-shelf bookcase.

g) We need three 250-gram cans of soup.

h) They are experts in building brick houses.

i) Mr. Smith bought a five-speed bicycle to his daughter yesterday.

j) The students wrote ten-page reports.

2. Fill in the blanks with one of the words in the list below to obtain compound nouns:

ache, air, central, clip, glasses, lace, path, post, table, washing

a) He put the tablecloth on the table.

b) The plane landed on the nearest airport due to damages.

c) He was wearing sunglasses because it was a very sunny and bright day.

d) She bought that necklace because it fitted her earrings.

e) He sent his letter by air post.

f) He wrote everything down on the clipboard.

g) Both of them had horrible stomach-aches.

h) She put the clothes in the washing - machine and turned it on.

i) It was too cold so they turned on the central heating.

j) That was the pathway to Chatham.

3. Fill in the blanks with a word from the list to form compound nouns:

bathroom, bottle, central, door, dish, dryer, fiction, heating, hair, mirror, money, shed, science, screen, top, pocket, shop, television, washer, window

a) He never has enough pocket money to buy himself whatever he wants.

b) He unscrewed the bottle top and then drank directly from the bottle.

c) Jane took the hair dryer to dry her hair.

d) They were watching the window shop fascinated while people were passing by.

e) He was fond of science fiction and he read everything of this kind.

f) After finishing his job, he closed the shed door behind.

g) The girl was watching herself in the bathroom mirror.

h) The house was warm and cosy due to the central heating.

i) The television screen was dusty and needed cleaning.

j) She put the dishes in the dishwasher and turned it on.

UNIT 15: SYNTHETIC AND ANALYTIC GENITIVE - PRACTICE

1. Put the apostrophe for the synthetic genitive where it is necessary:

a) The children's ball is in the garden.

b) She took her mother's car and left.

c) We gave the girls' books to their brothers.

d) The man over there's car is broken.

e) The boys' cups are in the sink.

f) The women's houses are well cared of.

g) The bird's feathers are red.

h) The girl's dress is blue and white.

i) The teacher's books are on his desk.

j) They took their friend's notebooks to learn.

2. Fill in the second sentence so that it has the same meaning as the first sentence:

a) I tried to find the children's toys.

b) The girls' cars were in the parking lot.

c) A girl's ribbon was left in the dust of the road.

d) Our cousin's house was quite roomy.

e) The book's cover was quite interesting.

f) My brother's room is cosy and warm.

g) My manager's cup broke the other day.

h) Their sisters' bicycles were in the garden.

i) She took her friend's dress to go to a dance.

j) I met my cousin's desk mate yesterday.

3. Correct the mistakes in the following sentences:

a) The boys' car was broken on the side of the road when I passed by.

b) They received their mother's letter yesterday morning.

c) She obliged their desk mate's sister by doing that.

d) We met our friend's sister in the park the other day.

e) Alice borrowed her brother's bike for a ride. She went to her friend's house three blocks south.

f) You took your sister's cap by mistake, didn't you? It wasn't intentional.

g) The two boys lived in their aunt's house for two weeks because their parents were out of the country.

h) I visited my grandparents' farm last week and I had a lot of fun with our neighbours' children.

i) Mary understood her teacher's explanation in class yesterday and therefore, she was able to help her friend's sister.

j) We gave them a lift in our father's car last evening.

4. Fill in the blanks using the words in brackets and the genitive:

a) The child was looking curiously at the bird's broken wing.

b) The leg of the table was broken and we couldn't do anything.

c) The summer sun was shining brightly over the fields of the region.

d) I saw the deer's eyes looking around with fear.

e) Your friend's sister's dress was smart.

f) The author's book met the expectations.

g) Young woman's solitude was moving.

h) The door of the room was open and we could look inside.

i) The colour of the shirt was strange and fascinating the same time.

j) The noise of the street could be heard from the last floor.

5. Turn the analytic genitive into synthetic genitive where it is possible:

a) The boy's book was lying on his desk during the class.

b) They saw the young man's new car in the street last night.

c) The book's title was exciting.

d) The colour of the walls was white and blue. → impossible

e) The wheel of the car came off. → impossible

f) That man's sorrows were beyond any imagination.

g) He forgot the key of the door on his table at home. → impossible

h) The young actress's name was already famous.

i) The desks of the classroom were new and clean. → impossible

j) The situation of the trial wasn't settled up. → impossible

UNIT 16: PROGRESSIVE TEST

1. Correct the mistakes in the following sentences:

a) The men are in the sitting-room and they are talking to each other.

b) The shelves are fool of jars of all sorts and all colours.

c) I got a lot of letters from my friends in the mountains during the last month.

d) Susan spoke to the children and brought them sweets.

e) They brothers-in-law greeted the bride when she entered the hall.

f) The mice ate the cheese in the pantry, I'm afraid.

g) He dropped the knives while laying the table for the guests.

h) The boys offered some flowers to their hostess.

i) The flies have come to the honey because they left the lid of the jar aside.

j) The gipsies settled their tents at the foot of the hill.

2. Fill in the blanks with the nouns in the brackets in plural form:

a) The children are playing in the park together with their friends.

b) When they left the classrooms, they left the doors and windows open.

c) The ones that saw the mice on the floor of the barn ran out screaming.

d) The street was full of men and women having lively coloured boxes in their hands.

e) The beaches with fine and golden sand were invaded by noisy people.

f) From the top of the hill, you could see the roofs with red tiles and smoky chimneys.

g) The dice showed that they lost.

h) Their yard was full of geese and ducks.

i) The sheep were black and big. The shepherds guarded them helped by three big dogs.

j) He was watching the fish in the aquarium and enjoyed their colours when three men came to him.

3. Fill in the blanks with one word from the list below:

blue-jeans, children, government, Mathematics, matters, people, police, pounds, stories, team, teeth, trail, trousers

a) The government has decided to approve that move.

b) Do the three pounds belong to you?

c) My favourite subject is Mathematics. Which is yours?

d) Where are my blue-jeans trousers?

e) People never understand such matters.

f) Police abandoned that trail. They have new clues.

g) The team won the match on Saturday evening.

h) He never believed the children when he heard all those stories they were saying.

i) They knew that they were in trouble when they saw police at their door.

j) He was a tall young man with big and white teeth.

4. Choose the right answer to complete the conversation:

a) Have you got some water, please? I'm really thirsty. – 2. No, I'm sorry, I don't have any.

b) Now, everything will turn back to order. 2. The police have come.

c) What do you think of the number of thefts in the area this year? – 1. The number of thefts has increased.

d) Who's that lady over there? – 1. That one? She's George's aunt's daughter.

e) How long did your trip take? – 2. It's been a five-hour trip.

f) I've just seen Andrew. He seemed extremely upset. – 2. Oh, don't you know? He's just lost his possibility of being elected president again.

g) I think we need more glasses for the reception, dear. – 2. No, darling we need fewer.

h) Is there any sugar in this house? – 1. No, I'm afraid there isn't any.

i) Is there any coffee left after the meeting? – 1. Oh, yes, there's a large amount of coffee, if you want some.

j) What would you like to serve, sir? – 2. I'd like some fish.

5. Fill in the blanks with one of the words given in the list below:

any, none, few, fewer, less, little, more, some, the, that, this, those, two

a) This car here has a lower consumption than that car there.

b) None of the students knew the answer to the question and the teacher was very disappointed.

c) I have seen fewer people in the show-hall for this play than the other night.

d) I'd like some tea, if you don't mind. Not much, just a little.

e) There's less understanding nowadays than it used to be before.

f) She ate the cake, I'm afraid. There's none left.

g) I need two pieces of meat not one, please.

h) There are few observations about that phenomenon, I'm afraid.

i) We need more information on the subject, to be sure.

j) They'd like some bread with their soup, auntie.

6. Fill in the blanks with one of the words or phrases given in the list below:

a coffee, a fish, a good education, a good health, a loaf, an iron, a noise, a wood, education, health, noise,

some bread, some coffee, some fish, some iron, wood

a) The people from table two would like some coffee.

b) Education is important to make your way through life. However, to acquire a good education means a lot of work.

c) She is very sensitive. She can't stand noise.

d) She wished her aunt to enjoy a good health. Her health wasn't what it used to be.

e) They woke up and listened attentively: a noise came from downstairs. One of them took a piece of wood from the pile next to the fireplace.

f) She chose to eat some fish instead of soup.

g) Marian was sitting on the terrace with a coffee in her hand and she was sipping the hot liquid now and then. She was watching some iron towers that could be seen in a distance.

h) They went shopping because they needed an iron to take care of their clothes. They also needed to buy a loaf.

i) It was just a wood but they managed to get lost.

j) He was watching a fish swimming towards the luxuriant vegetation on the bottom of the aquarium.

7. Fill in the blanks with one of the words or phrases given in the list below:

a glass, a loaf, a paper, food, foods, meat, meats,

some bread, some glass, some paper

a) He went to buy some glass to replace the windows.

b) The meats in this shop are always fresh. The butcher is a very attentive merchant.

c) She bought a paper and hurriedly opened it on page five to see the article about which everybody was talking.

d) Meat shouldn't be eaten so often, or at least that's what the people say.

e) There was a lot of food on the table and the four guests were wondering what was in their host's mind.

f) She needed some paper to print those invitations.

g) The child broke a glass while trying to pour some juice.

h) We need bread, I'm afraid, so Janice went out to buy a loaf. She must come back soon.

i) There are lots of foods in this shop. You can choose one with meat, if you want.

j) I need some paper to write down a few facts.

Table of Contents

UNIT 1: SINGULAR AND PLURAL OF THE NOUNS — 6

RULES TO FORM THE PLURAL OF NOUNS — 6

UNIT 2: SINGULAR AND PLURAL OF THE NOUNS - PRACTICE — 13

UNIT 3 – COMPOUND NOUNS — 21

I. GENERAL NOTIONS — 21

II. PLURAL OF THE COMPOUND NOUNS — 22

UNIT 4: SIMPLE NOUNS AND COMPOUND NOUNS PRACTICE — 24

UNIT 5: COUNTABLE AND UNCOUNTABLE NOUNS — 31

UNIT 6: DETERMINANTS OF COUNTABLE AND UNCOUNTABLE NOUNS 36

USE OF DETERMINANTS 41

UNIT 7: COUNTABLE AND UNCOUNTABLE NOUNS - PRACTICE 44

UNIT 8: COLLECTIVE NOUNS 57

GENERAL NOTIONS 57

UNIT 9: COLLECTIVE NOUNS - PRACTICE 61

UNIT 10: NOUNS + PREPOSITIONS FOLLOWED BY GERUND 65

GENERAL NOTIONS 65

UNIT 11: NOUNS + PREPOSITIONS FOLLOWED BY GERUND – PRACTICE 68

UNIT 12: NOUNS FUNCTIONING AS ADJECTIVES 73

| GENERAL NOTIONS | 73 |

UNIT 13: NOUNS FUNCTIONING AS ADJECTIVES - PRACTICE   74

UNIT 14: SYNTHETIC GENITIVE (SAXON) AND ANALYTIC GENITIVE (LATIN)   78

SYNTHETIC GENITIVE (SAXON GENITIVE)	78
A. GENITIVE FOR SINGULAR	78
B. GENITIVE FOR PLURAL	80

| ANALYTIC GENITIVE (LATIN GENITIVE) | 81 |

UNIT 15: SYNTHETIC AND ANALYTIC GENITIVE - PRACTICE   82

UNIT 16: PROGRESSIVE TEST   88

| KEY OF THE EXERCISES | 97 |

| UNIT 2: SINGULAR AND PLURAL OF THE NOUNS - PRACTICE | 97 |

ENGLISH GRAMMAR PRACTICE – THE NOUN EXPLANATIONS & EXERCISES WITH KEYS

UNIT 4: SIMPLE NOUNS AND COMPOUND NOUNS - PRACTICE   **103**

UNIT 7: COUNTABLE AND UNCOUNTABLE NOUNS - PRACTICE   **108**

UNIT 9: COLLECTIVE NOUNS - PRACTICE   **117**

UNIT 11: NOUNS + PREPOSITIONS FOLLOWED BY GERUND – PRACTICE   **121**

UNIT 13: NOUNS FUNCTIONING AS ADJECTIVES - PRACTICE   **124**

UNIT 15: SYNTHETIC AND ANALYTIC GENITIVE - PRACTICE   **127**

UNIT 16: PROGRESSIVE TEST   **132**

www.ingramcontent.com/pod-product-compliance
Lightning Source LLC
Chambersburg PA
CBHW070107080526
44586CB00013B/1222